THE STORY OF KATHERINE JOHNSON

A Biography Book for New Readers

Written by
Andrea Thorpe

Illustrated by
Sawyer Cloud

ROCKRIDGE PRESS

For Bianca, a smart and curious girl who loves to gaze at the stars and reaches for them, too.

Series Designer: Angela Navarra
Interior and Cover Designer: Darren Samuel
Art Producer: Samantha Ulban
Editor: Mary Colgan
Production Editor: Nora Milman
Production Manager: Michael Kay

Illustrations © 2021 Sawyer Cloud. Photography © IanDagnall Computing/ Alamy Stock Photo, p.49; NASA Image Collection/Alamy Stock Photo, p.50; NASA Archive/ Alamy Stock Photo, p.51.
Author photo courtesy of JT Thorpe.

Paperback ISBN: 978-1-63807-031-3 | eBook ISBN: 978-1-63807-146-4
R0
Printed in China

CONTENTS

CHAPTER 1

A NATIONAL HERO IS BORN

Meet Katherine Johnson

Katherine Johnson was a curious and smart little girl. She loved to explore the world around her and asked many questions about the things she saw. Young Katherine loved to learn, especially about math. Numbers were her favorite. Katherine loved numbers so much that she counted wherever she went. She counted the dishes in the kitchen. She counted the silverware in the drawer. At night, Katherine even tried to count all the stars in the sky! As Katherine grew older, her love of math grew, too. She could solve even **complex** problems easily. Soon, Katherine became known as a math **whiz**!

Katherine was an excellent student. She did so well in school that she skipped a few grades. Katherine graduated from high school at age 14. When she was 18 years old, she graduated from college.

JUMP IN THE THINK TANK

Does it surprise you that someone can become a national hero by doing math? What kind of hero would you want to be?

When Katherine was young, she did not know she would become one of America's best **mathematicians** and biggest heroes. She did not know her math skills would help **astronauts** get to space. At the time, Katherine was just a little girl who enjoyed math and spending time with her family in West Virginia.

> If you lose your curiosity, then you stop learning.

Katherine's America

Katherine was born Katherine Coleman on August 26, 1918, in White Sulphur Springs, West Virginia. She was the youngest child in her family. White Sulphur Springs is a small town in the Allegheny Mountains. One of the town's most famous places is the Greenbrier Hotel, where Katherine's father worked. Many famous

people and US presidents have visited this fancy hotel.

Katherine was born near the end of World War I. During this war, many countries, including the United States, fought against one another. Katherine grew up during the **Great Depression**, when many Americans, including Katherine's father, struggled to find jobs. America was also still **segregated** when Katherine was born. Black children like Katherine could not go to school with white children.

In 1915, three years before Katherine was born, the **National Advisory Committee for Aeronautics (NACA)** was formed. NACA was created during World War I to help make America's airplanes better. Katherine didn't know it yet, but she would grow up to work at NACA, helping make airplanes stronger and safer.

WHEN?

1914	1915	1918
World War I begins.	NACA is created.	Katherine Johnson is born.

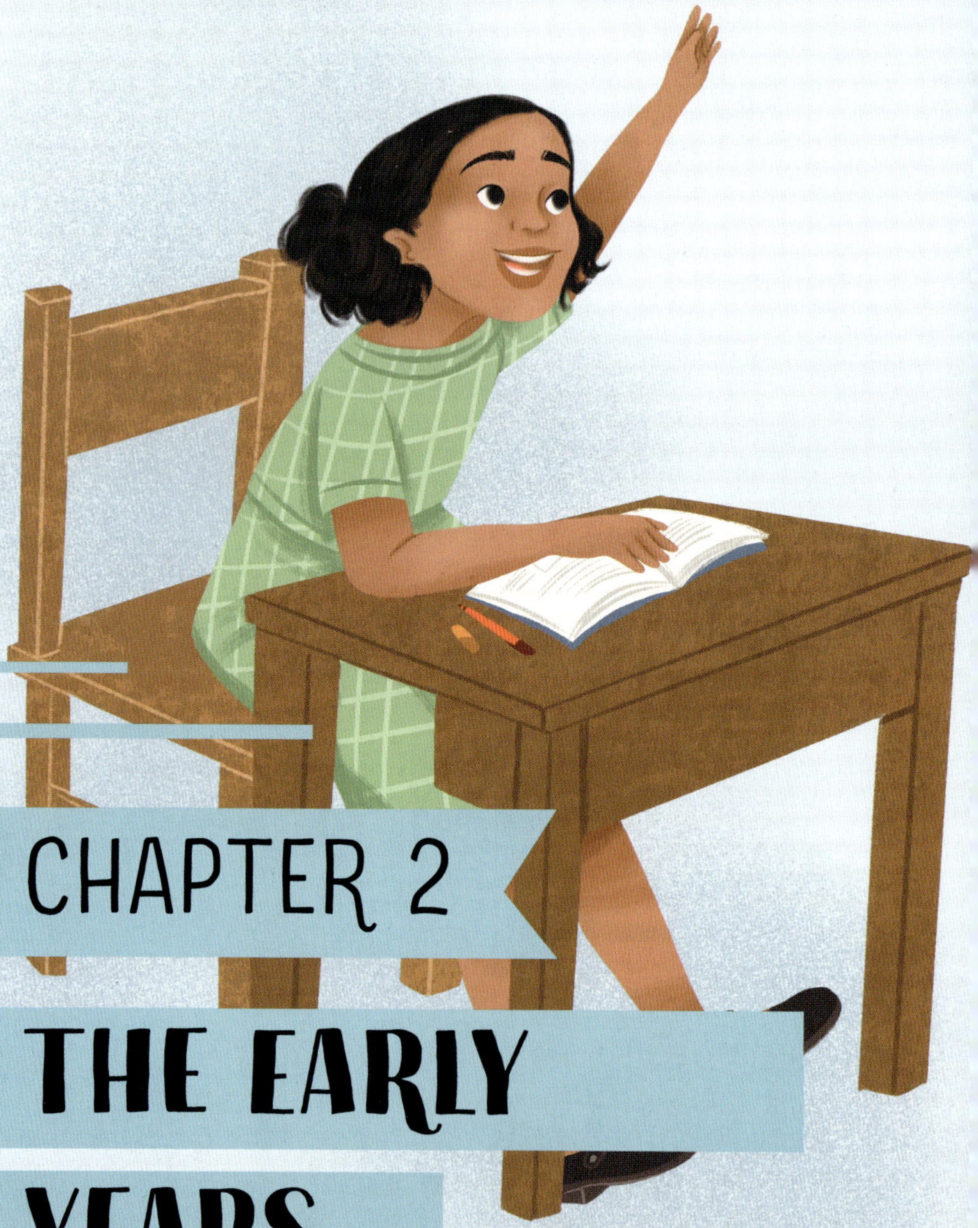

CHAPTER 2

THE EARLY YEARS

Growing Up Counting

Katherine grew up on a farm with her parents, Joshua and Joylette Coleman. Her mother was a wonderful teacher and her hardworking father was a farmer and **handyman** at the Greenbrier Hotel. Katherine also had an older sister named Margaret and two older brothers, Horace and Charles.

As a little girl, Katherine would sometimes slip over to her brothers' school and sit next to them in class. The boys' teacher, Mrs. Leftwich, let Katherine help them solve math problems. Katherine often got the answers before her brothers did. Mrs. Leftwich could tell that Katherine was gifted and wanted to learn. When Katherine was four years old, she started a special kindergarten class for Katherine and a few other children.

JUMP –IN THE– THINK TANK

Is there anything you might like about skipping grades in school? What might you dislike?

Katherine's father had attended school for only a few years, but he could solve math problems easily. As her father worked on the farm caring for horses, picking fruit, and cutting down trees, Katherine sometimes worked beside him. When he needed to use math **calculations** to design or build something, Katherine would do the calculations, too. She felt proud as she used math to help her father make and repair things.

Because schools in White Sulphur Springs were segregated, Katherine attended a school for Black children. She was an excellent student and skipped several grades. By the time she turned 10, Katherine was ready for high school, but there was no high school for Black students in her town. Katherine's parents wanted their children to get a good education, so they looked for a high school their children could attend.

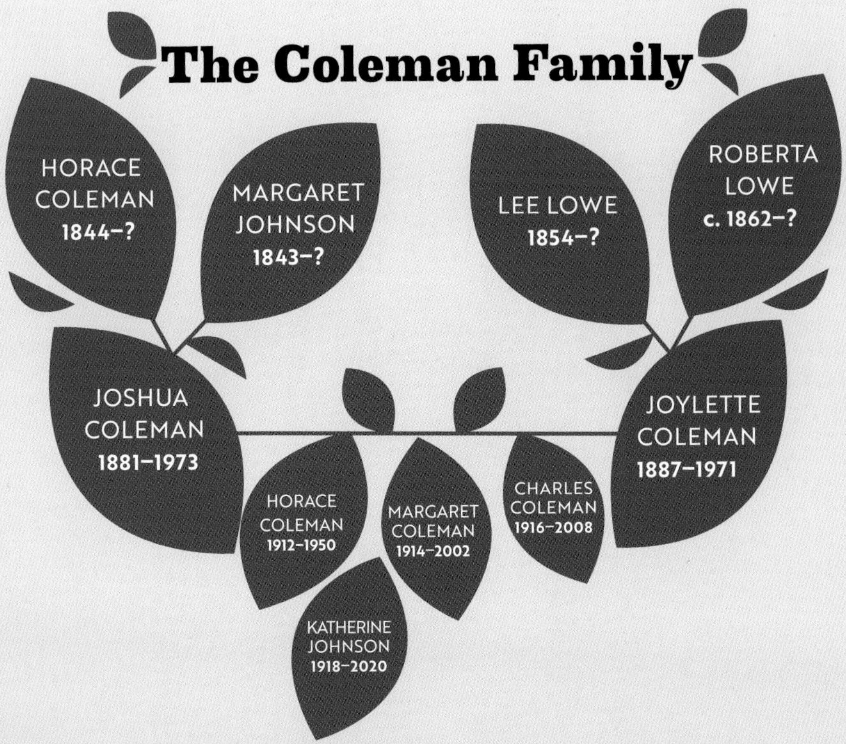

Higher and Higher

When Katherine's sister Margaret was ready for high school, her parents sent her to the West Virginia Collegiate Institute. The school was in a town called Institute, West Virginia, more than 100 miles away. Black students could get a high school **diploma** and a college **degree** there.

Katherine's parents wanted all their children to attend the West Virginia Collegiate Institute, so they moved to Institute in 1926. They rented a house and Katherine's father looked for work. He could not find a job in Institute, so he went back to White Sulphur Springs to work at the Greenbrier Hotel. Joshua Coleman missed his family, but he was **determined** to pay for his children's education. Katherine missed her father and sent him many letters.

Katherine and her siblings got jobs to help pay for school. During the summer, they worked as housekeepers and waiters at the Greenbrier Hotel. When the Great Depression began in 1929, many people could not find jobs and there was not enough food. Katherine's father did not lose his job, but sometimes Katherine's family could not get as many groceries as they needed. Katherine's creative mother learned to prepare delicious meals using fewer ingredients.

The Depression made life hard, but Katherine continued to do well in school. She was a friendly and **confident** student, and math was still her favorite subject. She enjoyed being around smart students who liked to use and talk about numbers. Katherine graduated from high school in 1933, when she was only 14 years old, and was accepted at West Virginia State College.

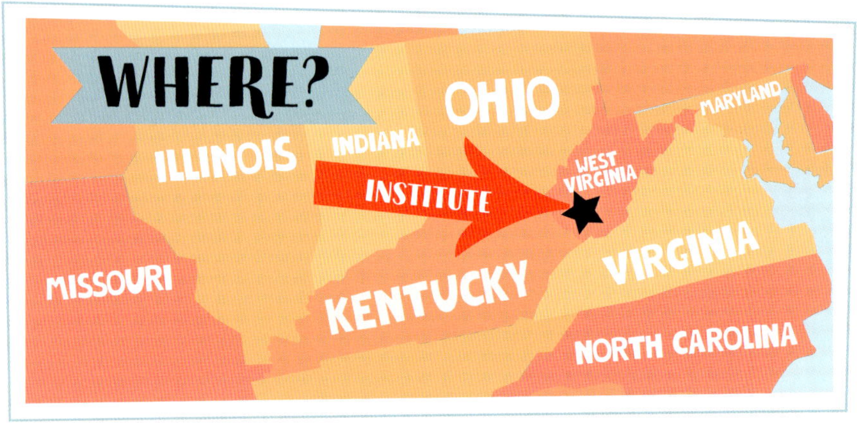

WHEN?

1926 — Katherine's family moves to Institute, West Virginia.

1933 — Katherine graduates from high school.

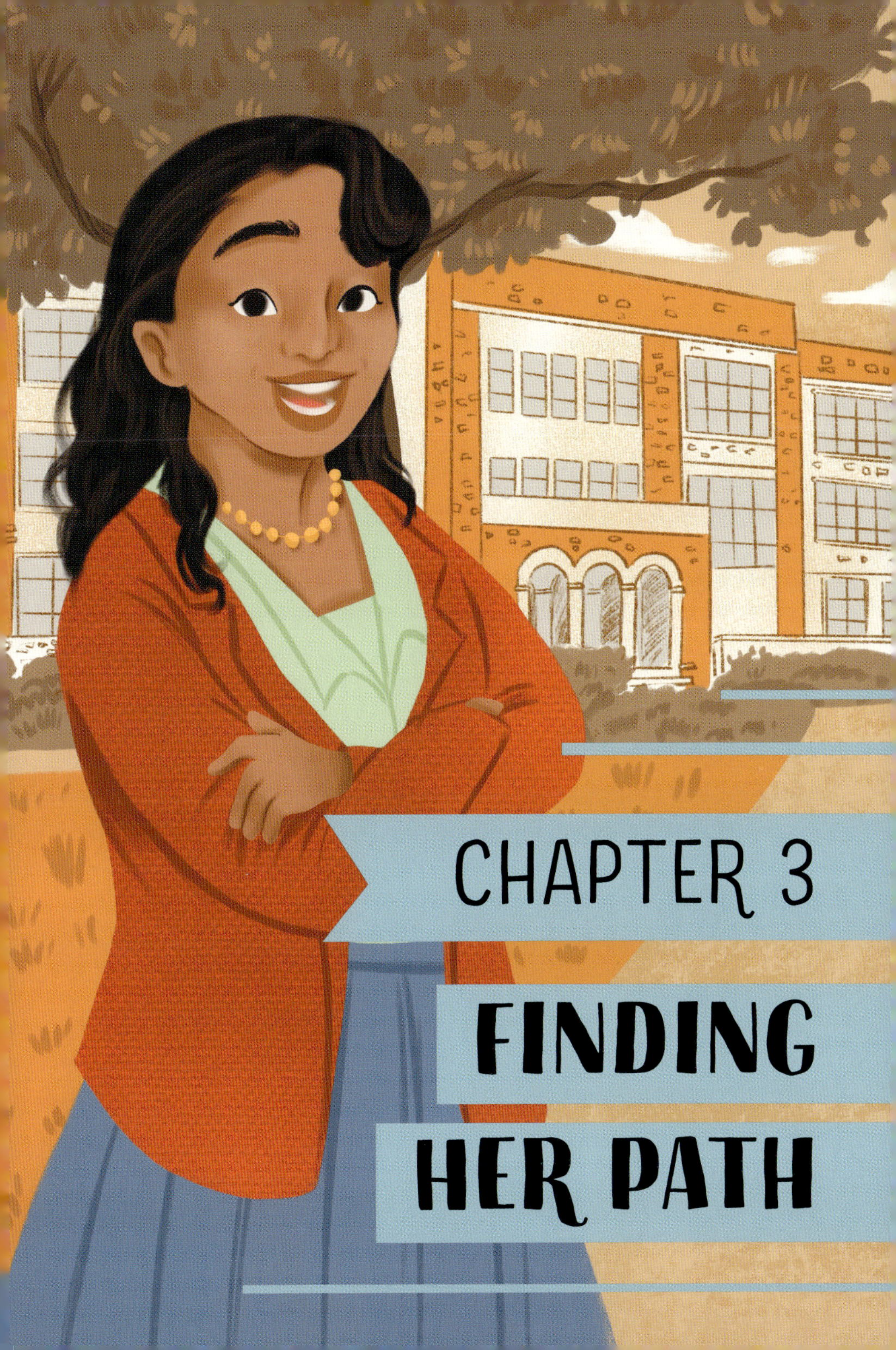

CHAPTER 3

FINDING HER PATH

With Honors

In the fall of 1933, Katherine became a student at West Virginia State College. Katherine took many classes and earned excellent grades in all of them. She still loved math, but she discovered that she also enjoyed learning and speaking French.

At the end of her first year, Katherine went back to her summer job at the Greenbrier Hotel in White Sulphur Springs. One day, Katherine was ironing clothes while a rich couple spoke to each other in French. The woman noticed that Katherine could understand what she was saying. One of the hotel's managers introduced Katherine to the hotel's chef, who was French. Every Monday morning, Katherine practiced speaking French with the chef. Her French was so good when she returned to school that her teacher thought she must have spent the summer in France!

Katherine decided to major in French. This meant that when she graduated, she would have a college degree in French. But she still loved math as much as ever. Dr. William Claytor was one of Katherine's favorite math professors. He encouraged her to think about becoming a **research** mathematician. Katherine completed all the college's math classes, including a special **geometry** class Dr. Claytor created just for her. Now she considered getting her degree in math instead of French.

JUMP IN THE THINK TANK

Katherine loved studying both math and French. What benefits could come from having more than one passion? What might be difficult?

When Katherine graduated from West Virginia State College in 1937, she was 18 years old. She never had to choose between French and math, because she had earned degrees in both subjects! Katherine's grades were so high that she graduated **summa cum laude**. This is a special honor given to students with the highest educational achievement in a class.

Stepping Out in the World

After graduation, Katherine was asked to teach French and music at a Black elementary school in Marion, Virginia. Katherine's students loved her fun and creative lessons. Katherine loved her students, too. They were eager to learn and worked hard.

Though Katherine was an excellent teacher, white teachers were paid more money than Black teachers. Katherine did not like that Black people were treated unfairly, but she was not **discouraged**. Katherine continued to work hard. She always told her students they were smart, talented, and important.

During Katherine's second year of teaching, she was asked to direct the school play. Jimmie Goble, the older brother of one of Katherine's students, agreed to help. Katherine and Jimmie became good friends and fell in love. They married in 1939.

In 1940, the president of Katherine's college asked her to become a **graduate student** in the math program at West Virginia University. The university had been a school for only white students, but it was looking for smart Black math students to **integrate** the university. Katherine still loved math, and she remembered that Dr. Claytor said she would make a good mathematician. She agreed to go back to school.

Katherine left her teaching job and became a **trailblazer**! She was one of the first Black students at West Virginia University. Katherine completed one year at the school, but she did not return in the fall. She was expecting a baby and she wanted to stay at home to care for her child. On December 27, 1940, Katherine and Jimmie welcomed their daughter. They named her Joylette after Katherine's mother. Another daughter, Constance, was born in 1943 and then a third, Katherine, in 1944.

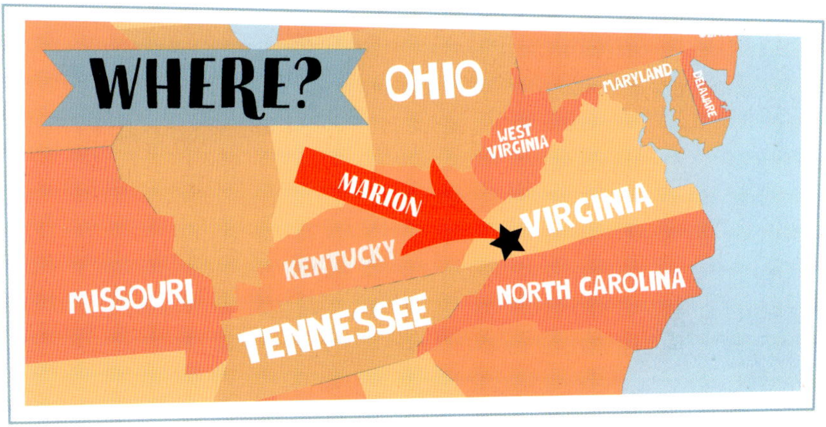

> "A good teacher helps students want to learn."

WHEN?

1933 — Katherine starts at West Virginia State College.

1937 — Katherine graduates from college.

1937 — Katherine becomes a teacher.

1939 — Katherine and Jimmie marry.

1940 — Katherine attends West Virginia University.

1940 — Katherine's daughter Joylette is born.

1943 — Katherine's daughter Constance is born.

1944 — Katherine's daughter Katherine is born.

CHAPTER 4
COUNTING PAYS OFF

Katherine the Computer

A short time later, one of Jimmie's relatives told Katherine about a special job at Langley Field in Hampton, Virginia. The National Advisory Committee for Aeronautics (NACA) was looking for Black women with math degrees. NACA was hiring these women to figure out, or **compute**, answers to math problems for the busy engineers. The women who did this job were called computers. In 1953, Katherine was hired as a computer for NACA. She had finally become a research mathematician!

When Katherine began working at NACA, electronic computers like the ones we have today did not exist. Back then, electronic computers were new and slow. Scientists did not trust the electronic computers' calculations, so Katherine and other women were hired to do all the math.

Katherine was disappointed to find that Black computers and white computers had to work separately. She knew their computing would be better if everyone worked together. Katherine had many questions, and she wanted to go to the engineers' meetings to get answers. Even though women weren't allowed to attend the meetings, Katherine bravely asked to go. Her questions were helpful and important, so Katherine's

JUMP IN THE THINK TANK

Why is it helpful for people with different ideas to work together on a project?

boss let her attend the meetings. After only two weeks, Katherine was **promoted** to a job in the Flight Research Division.

MYTH & FACT

MYTH: Katherine worked as an engineer at NACA.

FACT: Katherine worked as a computer at NACA. Her job was to solve math problems for the engineers.

Numbers That Fly

Katherine was excited about her new job. She would work with NACA's best engineers. One of Katherine's first tasks was to figure out why a certain plane had crashed. She studied the **data** from the plane. Katherine found that strong gusts of wind had caused the crash. She figured out that planes needed a lot of space around them and calm air to stop **turbulence**. Because of Katherine's work, new and safer flight rules were created.

Katherine and her family enjoyed living in Newport News, Virginia, where they moved to be closer to Katherine's job. The town was near Langley Field and close to family and new friends. Sadly, a few years after moving there, Katherine's husband Jimmie got sick. He did not get better, and in 1956, Jimmie died. Katherine and her daughters were heartbroken.

Katherine knew that Jimmie would not want his family to stay sad, so she and the girls kept busy. Katherine sang in the church choir and her teenage daughters joined the school orchestra. They felt better when friends visited and when they took trips to see relatives.

At NACA, things were beginning to change. Many countries, including the United States, wanted to learn more about space. By 1955, the United States and Russia were in a "Space Race." Both countries wanted to be the first to **launch** a **satellite**, send a man around the Earth in a spacecraft, and put a man on the Moon. The winner of this Space Race could say it had the world's best scientists and greatest space **technology**.

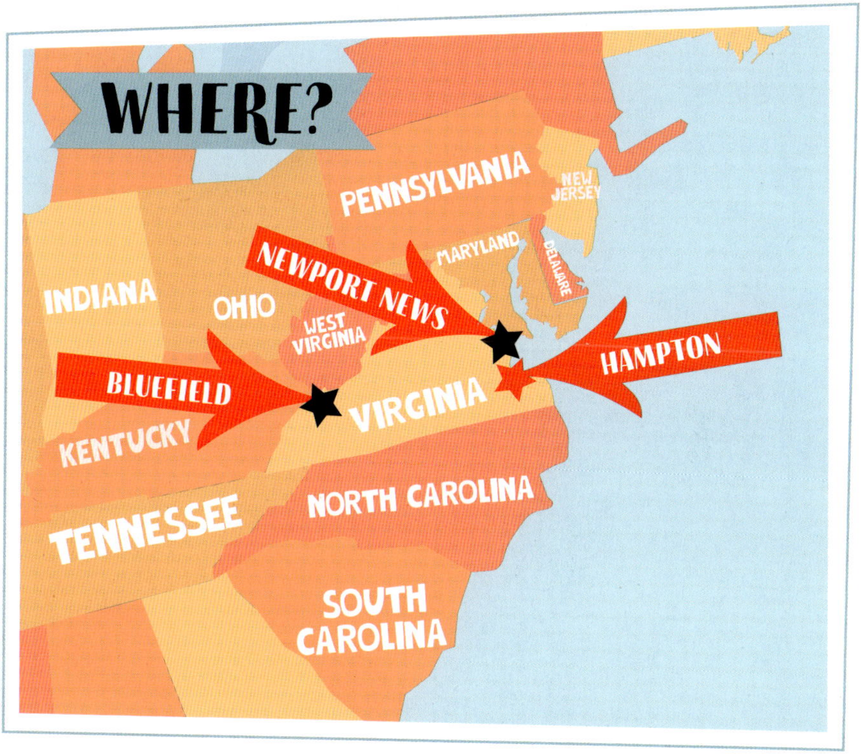

WHEN?

1953 — Katherine begins her job at NACA.

1955 — The Space Race begins.

1956 — Katherine's husband, Jimmie, dies.

CHAPTER 5

WORKING AT NASA

Project Mercury

In 1957, Russia launched a machine that traveled around the Earth. This satellite was named Sputnik. Americans were shocked! The US government thought it knew more about space than any other country and had hoped to launch the first satellite. NACA wanted Americans to reach space, and Katherine was ready to use calculations to help.

Katherine attended special NACA meetings and was asked to make drawings and charts about what she had learned. This wasn't hard for Katherine, because Dr. Claytor had taught her how to do this in college. Her work helped engineers learn more about space.

In 1958, NACA changed its name to the **National Aeronautics and Space Administration (NASA)**. NASA asked Katherine to help with a plan to send men into space, which they called

Project Mercury. Katherine was honored to work on such an important project. She was excited about using her math skills to help the United States jump ahead in the Space Race.

When she wasn't working, Katherine attended church choir practice. There she met a kind and handsome man named James Johnson. James and Katherine began to spend a lot of time together. They took walks and went to dances. Katherine and James fell in love and married in 1959.

In 1961, the new president, John F. Kennedy, made an announcement. By 1969, he wanted the United States to land a man on the Moon and bring him back to Earth safely. NASA was ready to take on President Kennedy's challenge, so Katherine was given a new task. She had to show the path a spacecraft should take to get an astronaut to the Moon.

Katherine on a Mission

NASA hoped Project Mercury would help the United States win the Space Race. NASA created new ways for astronauts to talk to engineers on the ground. It sent a chimpanzee on a test flight to learn how space travel affected living creatures. The chimpanzee came back healthy! NASA was almost ready to send a man into space, but in the end, Russia did it first. In April 1961, Russian **cosmonaut** Yuri Gagarin became the first person to fly into space.

NASA was disappointed but not ready to give up. It had already chosen a pilot named Alan Shepard to become the first American in space. In May 1961, Americans turned on their televisions and watched the astronaut soar into space. Alan stayed in space for 15 minutes and then came back down to Earth. His mission, Freedom 7, was a success!

In February 1962, John Glenn, a former **marine** test pilot, flew into space next. He made history as the first American to circle the Earth. Americans cheered from their homes as they

watched John's flight. His mission, Friendship 7, was perfect! His flight helped the United States catch up to Russia.

None of this would have happened without Katherine's work. She showed astronauts how to get to and from space. She made sure they would not get lost and could land safely. As she watched both missions, Katherine was excited but nervous. She had checked her calculations many times, but she could not relax until the astronauts had finally returned safely. Her numbers were right! Katherine smiled and wondered about her next project.

JUMP IN THE THINK TANK

The United States and Russia each wanted to win the Space Race. What good and bad things can come from countries or people competing?

> "I never needed inspiration to go to work. My work inspired me."

WHEN?

1957

Russia launches Sputnik.

1958

NASA is created.

1959

Katherine and James marry.

1961

Alan Shepard is the first American to fly in space.

1962

John Glenn is the first American to circle Earth in space.

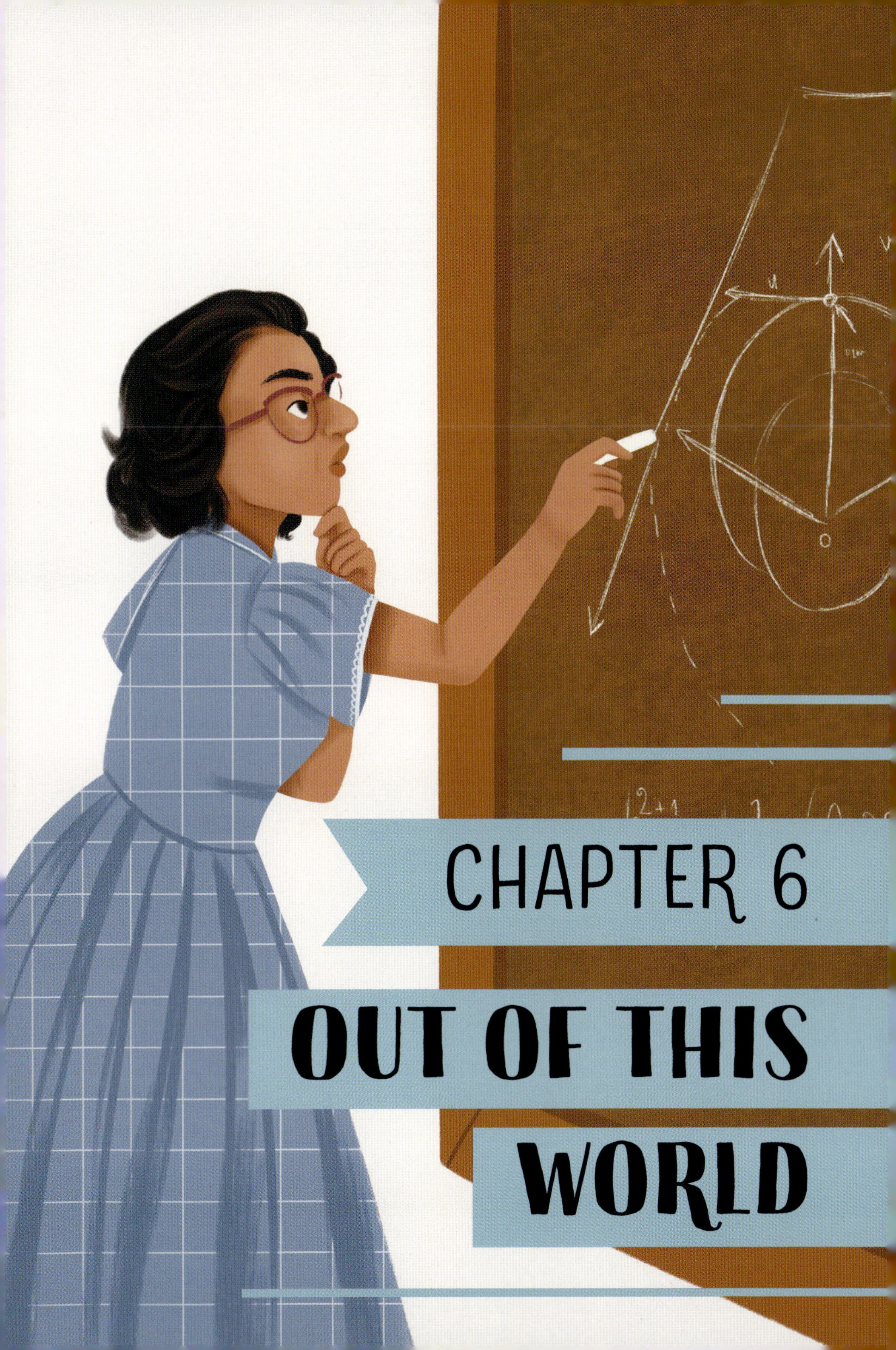

CHAPTER 6
OUT OF THIS WORLD

Into the Beyond

Project Mercury had proved that people could survive in space. NASA was now ready to send an astronaut to the Moon, so it created the Apollo program in 1963. Katherine joined the program and worked with engineers in the Space Mechanics Division. She figured out different paths to get to and from the Moon and also wrote reports explaining how to use the stars as guides.

Neil Armstrong, Buzz Aldrin, and Michael Collins were chosen as Apollo 11's **crew**. Now Katherine needed to show the exact path the astronauts should take so they would know where to land. This was harder to compute, because the Earth and Moon were always moving. Katherine also created a **navigation** plan for the astronauts to use in case of a space emergency.

On July 16, 1969, Apollo 11 headed for the Moon. Katherine was full of energy as she watched the liftoff. She was confident her calculations were right. When Neil Armstrong stepped onto the Moon on July 20, 1969, Americans cheered and celebrated. Katherine was happy, but she knew many more things had to go right for the mission to be successful.

The astronauts explored the Moon and returned to Earth on July 24, 1969. Katherine was thrilled. NASA had sent men to the Moon, and they had returned safely. The United States had won the Space Race by reaching the Moon before Russia!

To the Moon and Back

After Apollo 11, NASA sent more men to the Moon. In 1969, Apollo 12 made a successful trip to the Moon and back. In 1970, Apollo 13 was also expected to have a safe trip to the Moon, but the crew never made it there. On the way to the Moon, one of the spacecraft's air tanks exploded. The Apollo 13 crew canceled their Moon landing and made a dangerous trip back to Earth.

> "The whole idea of going into space was new and daring. There were no textbooks, so we had to write them."

JUMP IN THE THINK TANK

After Katherine retired, what do you think she missed most about working at NASA?

Years earlier, Katherine had created emergency plans for Apollo trips. Those plans included star charts to help the crew find their location in space. Katherine's calculations helped the Apollo 13 crew get back to Earth safely.

After Apollo 13, Katherine worked for NASA for 16 more years. She learned a special computer language called FORTRAN. It helped her understand how NASA's machines worked. When the space shuttle became the newest machine for space travel, Katherine came up

MYTH & FACT

MYTH: Katherine talked to the men on Apollo 13 and guided them back to Earth.

FACT: Katherine's charts and emergency plans helped the crew get back to Earth.

with calculations for its trips. In 1986, Katherine **retired** from NASA. She was 68 years old, but Katherine still had a lot of energy!

WHEN?

NASA creates the Apollo program.	Neil Armstrong walks on the Moon.	The Apollo 13 mission fails.	Katherine retires.
1963	**1969**	**1970**	**1986**

CHAPTER 7

LIFE AFTER NASA

A Hidden Legacy

Katherine still loved to teach, so after retiring she visited schools all over the country. She talked to students about her career and answered their questions about space. Katherine explained how math was used in everyday tasks like cooking and building. She encouraged the students to think about careers in STEM (science, technology, engineering, and math) and reminded them to get a good education.

Katherine was happy that she could spend more time with her family. When her grandchildren came to visit, she smiled and served her homemade applesauce. She laughed as she played puzzles and card games with her grandchildren. Katherine made up math problems for them, and they raced to see who could solve the problems first. She was always happy to help her grandchildren with their math homework, too.

When Katherine was much older, she received a special award. In 2015, President Barack Obama gave her the Presidential Medal of Freedom. This is a special award given to a US citizen who has worked to make the United States a better place to live. One year later, in 2016, a book called *Hidden Figures* was published. It was all about the work Katherine and her fellow computers had done at NASA. In 2017, *Hidden Figures* became a movie. That same year, NASA honored Katherine by naming one of their new research buildings after her. Now everyone knew what Katherine had done!

Katherine was happy to know other people were interested in what she had done during her long career. She was grateful to receive so many wonderful awards. Katherine was especially glad her family was there to celebrate with her. A few years later, Katherine Johnson died on February 24, 2020. She was 101 years old.

True Trailblazer

Katherine Johnson was an intelligent little girl who grew up to be an amazing trailblazer! She was a woman with many firsts. Katherine became one of the first Black students to integrate an all-white college. She was a great problem-solver who became one of the first Black human computers at NASA. At work, Katherine became the first woman to attend important NASA meetings. Throughout her life, Katherine always reached for the stars!

Katherine wanted to be the best, so she worked hard at every job she had. Because she was such an excellent worker, she was promoted many times. She knew women could make a difference in the world, so Katherine refused to be ignored. She was not afraid to ask questions and she always got answers. She encouraged others to ask questions, too.

JUMP IN THE THINK TANK

Katherine Johnson did many excellent things. Which one of her achievements do you think was the most special and why?

Helping others was important to Katherine. She loved talking to students about education.

> "I cannot recall a single day when I did not want to go to work."

Her unique life inspired them to think about ways to improve their own lives and their communities. No matter where she was or who she was with, Katherine Johnson pushed the limits and encouraged others to do the same thing. She lived a life that was out of this world!

WHEN?

2015	2016	2017	2020
Katherine is awarded the Presidential Medal of Freedom.	The book *Hidden Figures* is published.	NASA names a research building after Katherine.	Katherine dies at 101 years old.

CHAPTER 8

SO . . . WHO WAS KATHERINE JOHNSON?

Challenge Accepted!

Now that you have learned about Katherine Johnson's amazing life, let's test your knowledge with a who, what, when, where, why, and how quiz. Feel free to look back to find the answers if you need to, but try to remember first.

1 Where was Katherine Johnson born?

- A White Sulphur Springs, West Virginia
- B Marion, Virginia
- C Institute, West Virginia
- D Hampton, Virginia

2 How did President Barack Obama honor Katherine Johnson?

- A He named one of his daughters Katherine.
- B He declared a national holiday.
- C He named a town after her.
- D He gave her the Presidential Medal of Freedom.

3 **Why is Katherine Johnson known as a national hero?**

- A She fought in World War II.
- B She helped send astronauts to the Moon.
- C She became president of the United States.
- D She built a space station.

4 **What second language did Katherine learn to speak?**

- A Spanish
- B Japanese
- C French
- D Russian

5 **What is one of the subjects that Katherine taught to young children?**

- A Math
- B Art
- C History
- D Music

6 **How many children did Katherine have?**

- A 0
- B 1
- C 2
- D 3

7 **Who was Katherine's favorite math professor?**

- A Dr. William Claytor
- B Dr. Michael Jones
- C Dr. Richard Smith
- D Dr. James Kennedy

8 **What was the name of the project Katherine was asked to work on?**

- A Project Jupiter
- B Project Mercury
- C Project Saturn
- D Project Venus

9 **How old was Katherine when she died?**

- A 99
- B 53
- C 101
- D 67

10 **What did Katherine do as a NACA computer?**

- A She solved hard math problems.
- B She taught classes.
- C She fixed broken machines.
- D She worked as a secretary.

Answers: 1. A, 2. D, 3. B, 4. C, 5. D, 6. D, 7. A, 8. B, 9. C, 10. A

Our World

Katherine Johnson's work made our world a better place. Let's think about what her life has shown us.

→ Katherine asked to join the NASA meetings men attended. She showed others how to be brave by speaking out about unfair treatment.

→ Katherine used her math skills to help astronauts get to the Moon and back. She proved that Black women were smart, and they could use their knowledge and skills in math careers.

→ Katherine visited students all over the country and talked about her work. Katherine inspired young people to consider jobs in math or science.

JUMP IN THE THINK TANK FOR MORE!

Let's remember some of the things Katherine Johnson did and consider how her work affects the way we think today.

→ Katherine was an amazing student and an outstanding teacher. She loved to learn and share what she had discovered with others. What is something you already know and could teach others about?

→ Katherine was excited about going to work because she loved her job as a NASA mathematician. What good things can happen when a person enjoys what they do at work?

→ Katherine encouraged her students to work hard and ask questions. Why do you think she thought it was important for students to ask questions?

Glossary

astronaut: A person who travels into space

calculation: A mathematical way to solve a problem

complex: Having many different parts

compute: To use addition, subtraction, multiplication, or division to find the answer to a math problem

confident: To be sure you can do something

cosmonaut: A Russian who travels into space

crew: A group of people who work together in a spacecraft, aircraft, or ship

data: Facts and information

degree: A certificate that shows someone has finished college

determined: Focused on reaching a goal no matter what

diploma: A certificate that shows someone has finished high school or college

discouraged: Losing confidence or hope

geometry: A type of math that focuses on shapes and lines

graduate student: A student who has a four-year college degree and is studying to get a higher degree

Great Depression: A period of time in history during which people had little money to spend, work was scarce, and many businesses failed. It lasted from 1929 until the late 1930s and affected countries all over the world.

handyman: A person who does many types of repair jobs

integrate: To end segregation

launch: To send into space

marine: A member of the US armed forces who serves on land and sea

mathematician: A math expert

National Advisory Committee for Aeronautics (NACA): An organization that studied problems with planes and helped make flying more safe

National Aeronautics and Space Administration (NASA): The US government organization in charge of the science and technology of airplanes and space

navigation: How spacecraft, planes, and ships find their way from one place to another

promote: To move up to a higher or better job

research: The study of a topic in order to find new information

retire: To stop working in a certain career

satellite: Something that orbits a planet, star, or other object

segregate: To separate people, usually based on their race or skin color

summa cum laude: The highest educational honor a college student can receive

technology: Science or knowledge that is used to solve problems or create new tools

trailblazer: Someone who does something for the first time and guides others

turbulence: Rough air movement

whiz: A person who does something well and easily

Bibliography

Houston, Johnny L. 2019. "The Life and Pioneering Contributions of an African American Centenarian: Mathematician Katherine G. Johnson." *Notices of the American Mathematical Society Journal* 66, no. 3 (March 2019): 324–329. AMS.org/journals/notices/201903/rnoti-p324.pdf.

Johnson, Katherine, Joylette Hylick, and Katherine Moore. 2021. *My Remarkable Journey*. New York: HarperCollins Publishers.

Johnson, Katherine. 2019. *Reaching for the Moon: The Autobiography of NASA Mathematician Katherine Johnson*. New York: Simon and Schuster.

Acknowledgments

Thank you, Katherine Johnson! Her never-ending curiosity, outstanding accomplishments, and remarkable courage have been an inspiration to many. I'm thrilled to share Ms. Johnson's amazing story with young readers. I hope children will follow her example. May they ask many questions and bravely soar above and beyond their comfort zones!

I am extremely thankful for the love and support of my wonderful husband and my three terrific daughters. I was able to complete this project because they prayed for me and provided the quiet time I needed to research, think, and write. They also stopped by my desk to give me hugs and chocolate! Sweet family, I love you. Thank you for your love!

About the Author

Andrea Thorpe is a wife and the mother of three daughters. She has been homeschooling her children for 11 years. Before becoming a homeschool mom, Andrea earned a bachelor of arts degree in English and a master's degree in student personnel services. During her nine years in public education, Andrea worked as a classroom teacher and guidance counselor and was recognized as Teacher of the Year. In her spare time, Andrea enjoys hanging out with family and friends, searching for bargains in antique and thrift stores, and working on home décor projects.

About the Illustrator

Sawyer Cloud is a self-taught artist living in Madagascar, her native country. Passionate about the visual arts, she learned illustration through personal research and work experience. When not drawing, she is singing and wearing her favorite fairy costume. She lives with her family and her two pets, Arya the dog and Potter the cat. Find her at www.Sawyer.Cloud.